Main Street, 1876. Population, around 13,000.

HOUSTON

THE ONCE AND FUTURE CITY

HOUSTON

THE ONCE AND FUTURE CITY

by GEORGE FUERMANN

with photographs by BERT BRANDT

1971

DOUBLEDAY & COMPANY, INC.

GARDEN CITY, NEW YORK

4

For two natives
Julie and Walter

PREFACE

The text of this book, if not the work of the artists and photographers, is for the most part a complaint, with affection. Not always, of course, but much of the text finds faults; it accuses. It finds fault in our complacency about our present and our future. It accuses us of indolence toward correction—indolence and just plain indifference.

If I learned anything important about my city in writing this book, I am sure that what I learned applies to all great urban centers and may be called a law of urban growth: the greater the population the greater the step backward inherent in every step forward. As Piet Hein wrote in *Grooks 2:*

> We shall have to evolve
> problem-solvers galore—
> since each problem they solve
> creates ten problems more.

"Hell is a city much like London," Shelley wrote in 1839. In 1885 a Houston visitor of two months wrote to a friend, "Try to remember Bill, hell and houston both begin with a h." Cities have always contained elements of hell (although the Houston Chamber of Commerce published a booklet in 1915 titled, *A Glimpse of Heavenly Houston*). And man continues to deplore what William Blake long ago deplored: the "dark satanic mills" that despoiled England's green and pleasant land. The architect who designed Pandemonium, the high capital of Satan in hell, must have been the first urban planner, and man must now accept the dismal philosophy expressed by Pope in a letter to John Gay in 1727: "I have many years ago magnified in my own mind, and repeated to you, a ninth beatitude, added to the eighth in the Scripture: 'Blessed is he who expects nothing, for he shall never be disappointed.'"

A book is revealed as much by what it fails to say as by what it says. And much that I meant to say has been omitted. How, for one thing, Houston came to see the space scientists as

Houstonians rather than esoterics. The Beryl E. Minards lived at Seabrook, where in 1962 nearly everyone was speculating about the probable effects on the community of the scientists and others who would be moving to the proposed Manned Spacecraft Center. Four men, arriving from Virginia to look at houses in the area, were invited to have coffee with the Minards.

They chatted about school taxes, water bills, and the like until Mrs. Minard, struck by how cordial, how down-to-earth her guests were, said as much. "We were afraid you space people might have little antennas coming out of your heads," she said.

The visitors laughed, and then one got to the heart of the matter. "Those antennas," he said, "must be in the same place as the oil wells we expected to find in every back yard."

And the time, for another, in October 1965, when H. R. H. the Duke of Windsor arrived at the Warwick Hotel, where he was to stay while in Houston for a post-operative examination at the Texas Medical Center. He was given a list of four dinners from which he was to choose one. As he had stayed at the Warwick while recovering from surgery ten months earlier, the hotel's culinary staff knew something of the Duke's tastes. The four menus included such gastronome's pleasures as Coquilles St. Jacques, Supreme de Faisan ma Facon, Carre d'Agneau, and Crevettes Newberg.

The Duke read the menus, returned them with thanks—and asked for hamburger (two patties on a plank).

And the time Prince Rainier and Princess Grace, the rulers of the tiny principality of Monaco, were taken on a tour of the Astrodome by its grand panjandrum, Roy M. Hofheinz, an extraordinary and controversial man. "How would you like to have the Astrodome in Monaco?" Hofheinz asked.

"Marvelous," said Rainier. "Then we could be the world's only indoor country."

(Hofheinz once told a reporter, "I've spent more than a week in here without ever seeing daylight," meaning the Astrodome.)

And the book wants for nothing so much as the people themselves, the ones who give Houston a tang, a personality and a character of its own. Alberta Wilson, for one, who could be said to live and help live. "We love the seashore," she once said of herself and her husband, Charlie, "and wherever we go we look for treasures, mostly shells, but pretty rocks and stones, too. I think we started in 1930."

The collection of shells became ever larger and larger, and after thirty-five years it filled boxes in the attic, in closets, and in the garage. "We had so many shells we didn't know what to do," she said—but, in fact, she knew exactly what to do. In 1965 the Wilsons loaded up most of her collection of seashells and drove them back to the Galveston beaches, where so many of them had been found.

"We returned them for others to find," she said. Which is to say that Mrs. Wilson, for many years a kindergarten teacher, gave back to the beach the shells she had taken from it for thirty-five years—so others would find them. "We took about five hours spreading them out so as not to make it too obvious," she said. "The people were so excited. At first they couldn't believe it."

And the book says nothing of such altruists on the grand scale as John and Dominique de Menil, the gifted, philanthropic, highly civilized pair who came from France to make Houston a more graceful, a more benign place to live. Nor does it say much of the many others like the de Menils, foreign and native, who by their lives and deeds counter the urban sicknesses.

Not a word is said, though it was meant to be a long subject, of our troubled schools, which is merely one aspect of what is conveniently called the liberal versus the conservative mind. You measure a city partly with statistics, which are almost absent from the book—that we have 4300 miles of streets and more than a million motor vehicles moving over them, that we are badgered by more than a million telephones, that the highest point within the city limits is only ninety-two feet above sea level, and that it is eighteen miles across the main body of the city limits north to south and twenty miles east to west. But all cities long ago spilled over their city limits, making statistics partly artificial.

Something of the city could have been revealed in trifles—the gravestone concern's ad in the Houston *Post,* "Father's Day Special. 20% disc. on monuments, 10% on markers," and the sign in front of a new apartment house, "Your Subordinates Cannot Afford to Live Here." And if it is hardly essential, it is surprising to learn that Houston is second to none, or so a scholar told us, in using the word "chocolate" in place names. And to learn that our fire hydrants are painted orange and black because a 1902 graduate of Princeton decided so to use the university's colors in 1925, when he was the city's water commissioner.

The trouble is, the important things stick out when you evaluate a city. Dr. Lawrence Senesh, then an economist at Purdue University, came to Houston to lecture in 1966. "My very first impression of Houston," he said, "was that this is not a city for pedestrians. It was built for people on wheels. The pedestrian here is a nonentity, and yet I cannot imagine a city without pedestrians."

Indeed, Houston may be the poorest walking city in the world. So many of our distinctions are an embarrassment. And yet what G. K. Chesterton said of Americans describes Houstonians fairly well, most of us being "born drunk. . . . They have a sort of permanent intoxication from within, a sort of invisible champagne." And a German proverb on America also fits Houston, for in Houston "an hour is forty minutes."

Johnny Goyen, a city councilman, talked about Indians to some classes at the Horn Elementary School in 1963. He later received a letter from a ten-year-old girl who had been in his audience.

"I like to hear about the Indians," she said, "but next time you come will you talk about the plans for the future of Houston?"

HOUSTON

THE ONCE AND FUTURE CITY

Sam Houston, for whom the city was named.

■

The man for whom Houston was named saw it for the first time on April 26, 1837, barely three months after it was started in fact rather than in the minds of two land speculators. "Altho' I had a favorable opinion of this locality," Sam Houston wrote to a friend two days later, "I must confess that I am agreeably disappointed. It combines more advantages and is far superior in every point of view to any situation I have yet seen in Texas for the seat of Government, and commercial and mercantile operation." He estimated the population of the village, then the capital of the new Republic of Texas, of which he was the president, at fifteen hundred.

Could he have entered the city from the north 133 years later, when nearly two million more persons lived in Houston than when he first saw it, he would have been puzzled by two signs—one reading, "Houston City Limit"; the other, revealing one cost of unplanned municipal success, "Caution: Breathing May Be Hazardous to Your Health!" It was signed by the Harris County Pollution Control Board.

Sam Houston would of course have been nonplused by the success of his namesake. As his vanity shadowed him, perhaps he would not have let himself see that with each of many steps forward, his city had taken a step backward. Or he might have said that the evils he saw were common to all cities in the middle of the twentieth century, the extending result of what Henry James called "the horrible numerosity of society." That the city eagerly sought just what vexed James about the London of 1881 is the inexorable fate of cities, as natural as the course of the seasons.

"The time has been," Charles F. Morse wrote in 1893, "that if a man in a far Eastern State was to tell his friends that he was going to Texas, his friends would bid him good-bye with the same feeling as though he had told them he was going to commit suicide." So he wrote in his little book, *The City of Houston,* which was published when the city's population was around thirty-one thousand. The condition he complained of changed soon enough; the great population he yearned for was to come little by little, and then en masse. He would have been ecstatic could he have known that the population of his city, which he called "the foremost city of the grandest state of the greatest country on the face of the globe," would in 1970 be more than fifty times the size of the city he knew. No one counted the cost then, and since then it has been counted only in spasms.

Texans, though now to a much lesser extent the majority of Houstonians, tend to dilate their history, but Houston is too new, too recent-come, to be historic. Nor do we have any traditions of history, as London has from the seventeenth century onward been a traditional refuge from despotism and persecution, as Paris has through much of the same period drawn creators, as Alexandria has for centuries been an inspired host to wickedness. What are Houston's 133 years to history? London and Paris count two millenniums and Alexandria twenty-three centuries. Rome had existed for nearly twenty-six centuries before Houston was even an idea.

Nor is ours yet a historic city in a larger sense. "The years by themselves do not make a place historic," Simeon Strunsky has written. "It is men who give the color of history to a place . . . A city is historic, vitally historic, in which famous men have lived, dined, talked with their friends, or have written books and painted pictures or composed music . . ." Unlike American cities of even roughly the same age—say Chicago and San Francisco—Houston has few distinctions, little seasoning, in that sense. But for O. Henry, who lived here for only eight months in 1895 and 1896, no creator of distinction ever lived and dined and talked here. If our almost instant metropolis did not contain nearly two million people, its history would be immaterial.

The men who have colored Houston's past, and shaped its character and formed its sense of proportion, have been merchants, business men, and more recently the men who have benefited from the fortuitous presence of oil beneath so much Texas land. If few of them have been Babbitts, if they have rarely been booster types, nearly all have been chamber of commerce types—by no means distinctions without a difference. It has been our good fortune that our leaders have lacked the oligarchic cohesion of the Dallas leaders, which depends on more unity and less individualism than Houston's leaders can manage. Yet they almost always do manage, as they would say, "to get the job done." It has been our misfortune that most of the jobs they choose to get done are material; few are altruistic or humanitarian or even, in the larger sense, community.

We believe in private property and private profit, and so we lack zoning and enough park land and, until 1970, even a rudimentary housing code. And if we pay an unbelievable price for the absence of these benefits, which absences we call freedoms, then many of us think it well worth the price. We are little concerned about community rights but zealously concerned about private rights—which read, as a rule, property rights.

The cause of this extreme individualism is less the fading effects of the frontier, which departed reluctantly, than the almost midwestern insularity of our middle class—white, Anglo-Saxon, but not alone Protestant, for the Roman Catholic Church became an increasingly important influence here after World War II. Nor does our middle class live only in the suburbs. Neither the core of our city nor very much of the peripheral area has yet been veined or hemmed by slums. (A visiting architect once said of Houston, "You don't put your slums in one unsightly place. You spread them all over the city.")

We are new historically; our population is even newer. Hundreds of thousands of Houstonians have not been here for more than a generation. Most Houstonians do not go very far back, though of course that is changing. Take Mr. X., who is not hypothetical. He moved here from Boston in 1958. His circumstance is unexceptional in the wooded Memorial area, where he lives. He was born and reared in the East, his wife in Texas. Of fourteen families, including his own, living in his vicinity, only two of the twenty-eight adults were born in Houston, only five in Texas. The other twenty-three adults were born in other states, mostly in the South, Midwest, and East. But consider their children. The fourteen families have forty children; thirty-one were born here, four more were born elsewhere in Texas, and only four in other states and one in South America. The adults are immigrants; most of their children are natives of Houston.

This goes some way toward explaining the absence of a sense of community in Houston. You see two aspects of this lack of homogeneity in observations made by two disparate but worthy men, the one a youngish folklorist, the other a retired engineer who was the foreman of an important Harris County grand jury. One, H. B. ("Mack") McCormick, was writing in the preface to a pamphlet accompanying each of two recordings, produced in England, of the folk music of Houston. Peyton Bryan, the other, was writing to the editor of the Houston *Post*. A *Post* editorial opposing commercialization of Buffalo Bayou had reminded him of some lines from Whitman's "Song of the Broad-ax." "They could have been written about Houston," he said, and quoted them:

> The place where a great city stands is not the place of stretch'd wharves, docks, manufactures, deposits of produce merely,
> Nor the place of ceaseless salutes of new-comers or the anchor-lifters of the departing,
> Nor the place of the tallest and costliest buildings or shops selling goods from the rest of the earth,
> Nor the place of the best libraries and schools, nor the place where money is plentiest,
> Nor the place of the most numerous population . . .
>
> Where no monuments exist to heroes but in the common words and deeds . . .
>
> Where the men and women think lightly of the laws,
> Where the populace rise at once against the never-ending audacity of elected persons . . .
>
> Where the citizen is always the head and ideal, and President, Mayor, Governor and what not, are agents for pay . . .
>
> There the great city stands.

"Except, of course," Bryan went on to say, "Houston is not a city at all. It's a geographic term, describing a congeries of

The Manned Spacecraft Center: One way the astronauts trained to land on the moon.

villages, none of which particularly gives a damn about the 'audacity of elected persons' unless the audacity threatens its own serenity or property values. For Houston, above all, is a place to make money . . .''

Bryan described us as ''a congeries of villages.'' McCormick, writing nine years earlier, described us as ''an amalgam of villages.'' Houston, McCormick wrote, is ''less a city than it is an amalgam of villages and townships surrounding a cluster of skyscrapers. Each section of the city tends to reflect the region which it faces, usually being settled by people from that region. Thus the Louisiana French-speaking people are to be found in the northeast of Houston; the East Texas people in the northern fringe, which itself is the beginning of the Piney Woods; the German and Polish people are in the northwest Heights; and so on. . . . Each area surrounding the city has gathered its own, and each group has in turn established a community within the city. And so the city, which in itself has no cultural traditions, is rich in those it has acquired.''

Whatever we are, whether a cluster of villages or a city, we come to nearly two million persons living in an area that contained fewer than a hundred thousand (and Houston fewer than fifty thousand) in 1900. And like most other American metropolitan centers, we are content to be misgoverned exactly as we were governed in 1890, when Houston's population was 27,557. No one buys a 1970 automobile to install in it the motor from an early Model T Ford, but we seem quite willing to be governed that way. Yet an adequate form of urban political unit exists—the central metropolitan governing unit—but is widely shunned. It would save us time, money, and agony, yet none of us will hear of any departure from the status quo.

We do pull together in some things, obviously, but we know little of the accord that binds together, at least on the surface, the leaders of many cities. ''There is nobody here . . . worth a damn,'' W. P. Hamblen wrote to John P. Brady in 1867. ''I tell you this city is sorely in need of men. There is no doubt that she is dwindling into a one-horse concern.'' Hamblen and Brady were early leaders in Houston's attempt to become a seaport, although the city is fifty miles inland. Nearly a century later Houstonians were diverted by the spectacle of Jesse H. Jones, who was for many years known as Mr. Houston and who was simultaneously the Secretary of Commerce and the head of the Reconstruction Finance Corporation under Franklin D. Roosevelt, and H. R. Cullen, one of the richest men in the city's history, abusing each other over the issue of zoning. Jones favored it; Cullen opposed it. Cullen won, as the anti-zoning forces have always done in Houston. To zone the city, they say, would deprive them of their freedom.

We are a little drawn to what O. W. Firkins, writing of something else, called "pestiferous superlatives," one of which is that we are the most air-conditioned city in the world. As to that, Houston really is hundreds of thousands of air conditioners, perhaps millions counting the ones in most automobiles. Even our city buses and taxis are air-conditioned. For most of us, the noise of air conditioning soon becomes not inaudible so much as invisible to the ear.

What is surprising in a climate that begs for cooling and drying is that Houstonians are superlatively an outdoor people. And that means back-yard cookery and the links and the shooting ranges and the tennis courts even less than it means the beaches and the bay shore and the shores of innumerable lakes, from Lake Houston on the one hand, to the tens of thousands of tiny lakes at the tens of thousands of country places in surrounding counties. Most of the lakes were made by man on . . . well, on ranches. A meat inspector has ten acres in Montgomery County, to the north, and a half-acre lake for watering his livestock—four head of cattle. He calls it a "place"; his neighbors call it a ranch. Across Highway 149 from his place is a fifteen-acre tract, with house and small lake, owned by a longshoreman. The capitalist in the area, another Houstonian with decidedly slender means, has forty acres with a five-acre lake. And so it goes, a piece of the outdoors—one that appreciates substantially, and fairly soon, in value. As William Makepeace Thackeray said, "It is worth living in London, surely, to enjoy the country when you get to it," and so with Houstonians— the country or the bay or the beach.

Visitors often are surprised by, and many residents seem oddly reluctant about admitting to, one of the city's chief beauties. Though even the words "metropolis" and "megalopolis" sound hostile to nature, Houstonians are gardeners. And not alone because our climate invites things to grow, for once they start growing the same climate insists upon care,—care that is prudently given daily rather than in spasms of hopeful catch-up.

So we are air-conditioned, we are an outdoor people, and we are gardeners. Put those down to our weather. Most of us curse our weather, gladly and most of the time, even the considerable number of us who really like it. Most of us . . . but our weather is a subject apart.

The city lies almost astride the 30th Parallel—as does Cairo. Houston is farther south than the French Riviera, than Algiers and Baghdad. Houston, in fact, lies partly in the same latitude as the Sahara.

Weather is what the skies are doing right now; climate is what the skies have done for a long time. It gets hot and wet and humid in Houston, and sometimes all three at once. That's weather; unforgettable weather. But the city's climate is memorable for its excesses rather than for its pleasures, even its glories. Houstonians talked for decades about the great snowfall of February 14, 1895. It measured twenty-two inches. A twenty-two-inch snow is only slightly more of a piece with Houston's climate than it would be, say, with Death Valley's, but the snowfall was the focus of the people's weather recall until after World War I.

Winter, the season Houston gets the least of, is the most benign of the four seasons—with one often shocking exception. That is the norther. Like oysters, the norther is at its best in months containing an *r*, but its great furies come in the winter. "The meteorological pride of all Texas, east, north, south, and west, is the norther—the Texas norther," J. Frank Dobie wrote. "It comes so sudden and soon that old Judge Clark used to always go provided with both a fan and an overcoat."

Cold winds blow down across the top of Texas, pushing fast across most of the state, sometimes reaching down into the lower Rio Grande in southernmost Texas. These cold waves are the northers—blue northers or wet northers or dry northers. What distinguishes a norther from a plain cold wave is the sudden, dramatic drop in temperature. Most northers are preceded by heralds: the still, sultry air; the scent of sulphur or burning hay or charcoal; the haze, slowly, ominously obscuring the sun. Birds and beasts almost always know beforehand; often man can tell. Then, suddenly, the temperature drops and sounds break the stillness, first a low soughing of the wind, then bedlam as the fury commands the city.

Arriving in Houston in 1873, the Yankee journalist Edward King was at once introduced to the norther, "which came raving and tearing over the town, threatening, to my fancy, to demolish even the housetops. Just previous to the outbreak, the air was clear and the sun was shining. . . . It was glorious, exhilarating, and—icy."

Mark Twain once said: "When a man is accustomed to 100 in the shade, his ideas about cold weather are not valuable." That northers do seem a lot colder than the thermometer proves them to be owes to their swift arrival; a norther can drop the temperature forty degrees or more in a few hours. A magazine published for employees of the Humble Oil & Refining Co.'s Baytown refinery printed a full-page warning in January 1957: "Although the weather may be warm when you go to work, it's a good idea to take a top coat along to guard against a sudden drop in temperature."

A Minneapolis girl came to Houston some years ago to spend Christmas with an elderly aunt. During the days before Christmas the little girl spoke often and sadly of the absurdity of a Christmas without snow. At length her aunt's patience gave way. "Honey," she said, "whatever made you think that Jesus was born in a snowstorm?"

The first Christmas, of course, was by no means white, and to that extent most Houston Christmases have been traditional. Indeed, Houston has had but one white Christmas of sorts in the twentieth century. The city received a two-inch snowfall on December 21 and 22, 1929; a little snow was still visible on Christmas day. But as a rule roses bloom and the redbird sings his traditional spring song at Christmas time in Houston, where the day itself may be filled with sunshine.

The nineteenth century, however, is known to have given

Houston at least one authentic white Christmas. "Snowballing on Main Street!" the editor, Edward H. Cushing, wrote in the Houston *Telegraph* of Christmas in 1859. "Our fingers are tingling as in the boyhood we knew farther North; all hands had a hard time running the snowball gauntlet up Main Street this Christmas."

But call our climate semi-tropical. A Minneapolis land company printed a broadside in 1907 to advertise a land excursion to Houston. The broadside compared Minnesota and Houston winters with relish. "Take a trip with us," it said, "to where happy farmers are picking strawberries every day, while we fellows are suffering 20 below zero."

Sometimes Houston's winter skips, like a flat stone cast on the surface of a pond, into a miragelike fifth season called Blackberry Winter. It is a brief interlude of satisfying weather between spring's budding and shooting and summer's furnace. Blackberry Winter is an old friend of the East Texas region, which it favors by dropping in for a day or so most every year, and now and again it spreads to the Gulf. Blackberries are ripe and choice, burgeoning in the city's vacant lots and in the country's fields. By the time the people have decided what to do about the welcome visitor, turning out light coats and sweaters just put away, Blackberry Winter is gone.

Houston's rain season may run from January to December. It depends. E. Bagby Atwood's *The Regional Vocabulary of Texas* shows that weather leads all subjects in the number of synonymous words and phrases. Perhaps that is true of all states, but these words and phrases mean the same thing in Texas—a torrential rain: chunk floater, chunk mover, clod roller, cloudburst, cob floater, dam buster, downpour, duck drencher, dumplin mover, flood, flash flood, frog strangler, gully washer, pourdown, stump mover, toad strangler, trash floater, waterspout, and many more.

So copious a vocabulary for a hard rain was inspried by a history of hard rains. Sometimes it rains and rains in Houston (and sometimes you despair that it may never rain again). It rained thirteen days in a row, which was a record, in June and July of 1963. Rarely does it rain a gentle rain; rarely does it

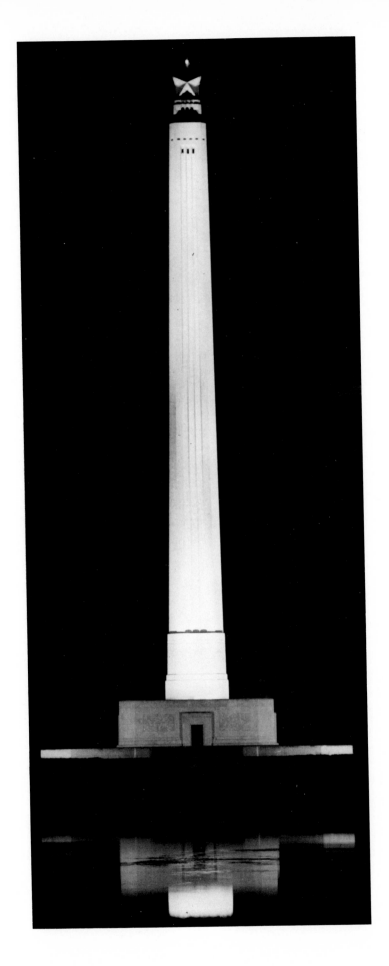

The San Jacinto Monument,
commemorating the battle
in which Texas won
its independence from
Mexico in 1836.

Page one of the Houston *Post* of January 13, 1901, announcing the Spindletop discovery well—a "SOLID STREAM OF PETROLEUM" that initiated a substantial part of Houston's future success.

rain just right. The rain in Houston falls mainly from buckets. The annual record is 72.86 inches, or a fraction over six feet, which fell in 1900, the year of the great Galveston flood, and again in 1946. The driest year was 1917, when only 17.66 inches of rain fell in twelve months. The city's normal rainfall is around 45 or 46 inches a year.

Rain means mud, for which Houston was celebrated during its first fifty years. The *Telegraph and Texas Register* called Houston a mudhole before the city even existed. Ezekiel Cullen, speaking to the Third Congress of the Republic of Texas, called Houston "that wretched mudhole." And in the 1870s and later, the people of Galveston, whose city was then larger than Houston, called Houstonians "mud turtles."

"Houston had the reputation of being the muddiest town in Texas and I guess we deserved the honor," Dr. E. N. Gray wrote in 1940, in his *Memories of Old Houston.* In the winter of 1879–80, he went on, "it rained three months without missing a day. Signs were put up all along Main Street bearing the warning: 'Keep out, no bottom here.' Finally it got so bad no vehicle could venture out. When anyone died the body was carried by hand to a street car track and then [by street car] to the entrance of Glenwood Cemetery whence it again had to be carried by hand to the grave."

"Hell hath no heat like heavenly Houston," Carl M. Brownfield, that well-tempered provoker of tranquil minds, wrote in an excess of alliteration. That may be an exaggeration, but Houston seems to have been the birthplace of what came to be called the Never-Sweat Set, whose members drive between air-conditioned houses and air-conditioned offices in air-conditioned automobiles. And Houston was the first city in the world, and is so far the only one, to build an air-conditioned baseball and football stadium. One of the most remarkable structures in the world, it was built by Houston's weather—the rain, the heat, the humidity—as much as by the extraordinary man who got it built and who leases it.

Houston's heat is the subject of a poem written long ago, before air conditioning. The author may have been George Phair, and the first and last verses are:

"How delightful!" said the stranger as he crossed the
  River Styx,
And he calmly took a stroll upon a pave of red-hot bricks;
And the devil saw him do it and it stung him to the core
That a stranger should be happy on that super-heated shore.

"Tell me, stranger, tell me truly, I implore,
Why do you like the climate on my super-heated shore?"
And the stranger gaily chuckled and responded in his mirth:
"I played ball in Houston, Texas, when I roamed upon
  the earth."

No one has written so wisely about Houston weather as W. D. Bedell, an editor of the Houston *Post*, who has called Houston a crossroads of the weather. "Here we can have Dallas weather or Caribbean weather or Colorado weather or Arizona weather," he wrote. "Houston gets more Caribbean and Gulf of Mexico weather than any other major Texas city. That is the steam bath kind of weather. . . . That is the weather that Houston has most of the time . . . that it fights off with cold drinks and featherweight clothing and air conditioning."

The old books on Houston say nothing of the steam bath kind of weather, not a word about our hurricane season in July, August, and September. Reading the old books, you gather that the climates of Houston and heaven are in fact one. Indeed, a book titled *A Glimpse of Heavenly Houston,* published in 1915 by the Chamber of Commerce, speaks of "the tang of the North winds that sweep down from the Rockies, mellowed by the balmy air of the Gulf of Mexico." And Andrew Morrison, in *The City of Houston,* published in 1891, says that "here truly is the enchanted summer land." A Houston motto in 1900 was, "Where the Mock Bird has no sorrow in his song, no winter in his year."

Houston's climate shows many faces. "But [the steam bath kind of weather] is not all the weather Houston has," Bedell went on to say. "The best is the Colorado weather. . . . When it gets to Houston words aren't enough to tell what heavenly weather it can be. The sky is painted water color blue and the air takes on a dry clarity that makes houses and trees stand out sharply, that makes just breathing a pleasure. When it

The Little Mecom Fountain, on the block north of the Warwick Hotel.

comes after the trees and grass are green . . . Houston is so beautifully beautiful it almost hurts."

Houston's night skies often seem higher and more handsome than most, and more newcomers, those who have lately known other skies, than natives feel this difference and wonder at it. The effect is puzzling, but the land's flatness and some quality of the night air, which can be surprisingly spare and clear—as though Houston were far above rather than nearly level with the sea—may account for it. When the clouds form so as to make a canvas for the sun's pinks and roses and deep saffrons, the show begins with our swift sunsets. And the air's effect on a rising moon, dilating it fantastically, can be stunning.

Houston's daytime skies can put on a quite different show: panzer divisions of clouds, gray and black and ominous, arrive hurriedly in counterfeit caprice, presaging the end of the world, or at least Houston's doom. Lights come up all over the expectant city, which quiets a bit for once. But as a rule the surly clouds deliver only a downpour on this section or that—a fast, whole-hearted, no-nonsense gully-washer—and often one unheralded by the weather bureau. But these are mainly summer shows, and each may impart to the city a brief, grave beauty.

Houston is flowers, millions of flowers. Our wealth of trees and shrubs and flowers owes to our semi-tropical climate. A legend says that Houston gets really cold only once every ten years, and the legend is close to fact. So we have a three-season option on the outdoors and an option on winter that we take up when we can, which is often. We have nearly a twelve-month outdoor climate.

Houston is Texas, and Texas is weather of almost inconceivable variety, as shown by one headline on page one of the Houston *Post* of September 11, 1955:

COLD WAVE IN N[orth] TEXAS;
TROPICAL STORM IN GULF

Mody C. Boatright, in his *Tall Tales from Texas,* lets Joe tell the story. A cowboy, he tells of a fellow who dove into a deep swimming hole. But the hot Texas sun dried up the water before he hit it. He didn't break his neck, though, because a sudden Texas rainstorm filled the hole. When he came up for air, however, his head got frozen tight in the ice, thanks to a norther. Joe added, "Leastwise that's what he used to tell, but he was such a windy that you never knowed when he was tellin' the truth and when he was tryin' to load somebody."

Texas weather has ever been the despair of weathermen. J. Frank Dobie wrote about one weatherman of more than a century ago. He was called Old Prob, and he came to Texas from the North. At last he decided to return after years of trying in vain to foretell Texas weather. He was asked to make one last weather prediction.

"For Texas," Old Prob said, "it will be hot as hades, er cold as flugens, as wet as a drowned rat, er as dry as a dried apple dam, jist whichever it damn pleases."

A tank—a reservoir of crude oil, one
of many hundreds in the area.

A detail of the dome grid of the Harris County Domed Stadium—the Astrodome—during construction.

■

Here, the New York *Daily Graphic* said in a long article about Houston, "a man can go into a drinking saloon and on slight provocation and very short notice get up almost any sized fight he wants." That was in 1880. Nearly a century has intervened since then, but the only way the condition has been altered is to have become intensified. For murder will out here. We laugh self-consciously about it, when we do not weep; we read and approve of editorials headed: "Houston Murder Rate Shameful" (1967) and "Shameful Record" (1968); but one marvels that we will not try—at least *try*—to oppose this condition, as Miami has, as Chicago has. A few have been moved to write verse about our peculiar affliction. That is all. The anonymous "Houston Song" suggests an open season on husbands:

> "I miss my husband so!"
>   The woman cried;
> And so just one more shot
>   At him she tried.

A limerick, more revealing, was written in 1958:

> In Houston we feel no aversion
> When others are casting aspersion;
>   We never mind much
>   The murders and such—
> We take them as week-end diversion.

But Arthur C. Evans's parody of Humbert Wolfe's parody of Housman is specific:

> When lads have done with labor
>   In Houston, one will cry,
> "Let's to the tavern, neighbor,"
>   And t'other answers "Aye."
>
> So this one clubs his brother,
>   And that one clubs a lad;

And somewhere someone's mother
Pumps lead at someone's dad.

In Houston, where the suds, men,
Foam blood-flecked to the brim;
In Huntsville, of a sudden,
The lights are briefly dim.*

Perhaps there is something in the air, or in the water. In 1957 we led all the rest, having the highest per capita murder rate in the nation. This grisly distinction was soon lost, but what Houston needs in this respect is to lose Texas. Texas customs and practice make it easier for a murderer to escape punishment than in any other state. We give a man five years in the penitentiary for "unlawful manufacture of intoxicating liquor," or operating a still, and four years for murder, to note but one pair of convictions upheld in the same year by the Texas Court of Criminal Appeals. But suppose that a murderer is unlucky enough to receive a 199-year sentence; he may apply for a parole after serving fifteen years, which may, in fact, be served in nine years with time off for good behavior.

Any Texan may own a pistol—the insane, the drug addict, the alcoholic, anyone. Two hundred and four persons were murdered in Houston in 1966, or fifty-eight *more* than were murdered in all of England in 1965. London, whose population is many times larger than Houston's, and which is much more densely inhabited, annually has fewer than half as many murders as Houston does. "And public indifference to the homicide toll lets murder stalk the community unhindered—and with implied public acceptance," the Houston *Post* said in an editorial in 1967. "The public is silent. There is no outcry against murder. And silence gives consent."

The frontier left us at last, but the hallucination lingers. The 204 murders in 1966 increased to 287 in 1970. Certainly violence is deep-etched in our past. In 1838 the diarist John Hunter Herndon called Houston "the greatest sink of disipation [*sic*] and vice that modern times have known." Francis C. Sheridan, a young Irishman in the British diplomatic service, saw Houston in 1840, when he wrote, "I heard and read of more outrage

*The electric chair in Texas is at the state prison in Huntsville.

and blackguardism in that town [Houston] during my stay on the coast committed there, than throughout the whole of Texas." The Methodist Bishop J. O. Andrew, who saw Houston in 1843, wrote, "Beyond all doubt, there is a great need for a deep, a thorough, a sweeping revival of religion in Houston." And more than a century later, in 1952, the evangelist Billy Graham would say, "Most Houstonians will spend an eternity in hell."

There is something in the water, all right. But the subject now is not murder but the Port of Houston and the Houston Ship Channel, without which Houston would be of little consequence.

Houston, the nation's third-ranking port, we say,—usually without having any idea of the limitations of the boast. The fact is true enough for most years, but it needs to be explained, as much to inform Houstonians as others. "Houston's claim [to then being ranked the second port in the United States] has been rather tenuous," the Houston *Post* said in an editorial in 1956, "based largely on the vast movement of petroleum and its products through the port . . ." In short, the Port of Houston moves little of what goes into the ranking figures of most ports, called dry cargo, but moves much bulk crude oil, refined products, and petrochemicals. And so, perhaps no other port city anywhere has less of the flavor and romance of the sea than the Port of Houston.

To begin with, the port itself is fifty miles from the sea. Buffalo Bayou and the San Jacinto River—the bayou of the bison and the river of St. Hyacinth—are the first reasons for the city's success, as Buffalo Bayou was in the beginning the reason for the city's site. The long development of the port from little more than a fancy into one of the dominant ports of North America has been an astonishing revelation of the effectiveness and determination of men, and fortune played little part in the story. But the port remains fifty miles from the sea—"with its artificial canal in a meadow," Katherine Anne Porter wrote in *Ship of Fools,* and the Houston Ship Channel did pass mostly through meadow land in 1931, the time of the novel.

It is by no means uncommon to hear a resident, as well as a visitor, complain that he has never seen the port, that he cannot even find it. Of course, he is looking for a port that looks like a port, and his annoyance recalls a madcap book, *On a Mexican Mustang Through Texas,* written by Alexander E. Sweet and J. Armoy Knox and published in 1883. "I had heard about Houston being a seaport," the authors say, "but I thought it was a joke. . . . I yearned to see that seaport, even if I had to employ a detective to hunt it up. I knew it was in Houston concealed somewhere, but I was afraid it would be removed to a place of safety before I could see it."

However that may have been, however much our port may fail to season the city with the tang and the traditions of the sea, the city's material success has for the most part followed, not led, the development of the port and the Houston Ship Channel. Houston's quick growth between 1940 and 1960, when its population rose from twenty-seventh to sixth place among American cities, owed to the linking of three things: the ship channel; immense resources of oil, natural gas, sulphur, lime, salt, and water; and the fact that the product of one chemical plant is often the raw material of another. This combination created on the banks of the ship channel one of the world's greatest concentrations of petrochemical industries.

It also created important sources of pollution, another instance of a step forward in which a step backward was inherent. Buffalo Bayou itself, once the city's most visible natural gift, became an open sewer. It was once a beauty, the land's benediction. A traveler who wrote of the bayou nearly ten years before

The earliest known sketches of Houston were made in December 1837, when the town was barely less than a year old, by Mary Austin Holley. The larger structure is the capitol of the then Republic of Texas. (*Courtesy the University of Texas*)

Houston existed called it a "most enchanting little stream." Many early travelers noted Buffalo Bayou's "appearance of an artificial canal" and its "strong resemblance to a canal," which in good time it would become. "This bayou Houston hopes one day to widen and dredge all the way to Galveston," the journalist Edward King wrote in 1873, adding that "its prettiness and romance will then be gone."

The melancholy prophecy of that last statement was revealed a century later when a commissioner of the Federal Water Pollution Control Administration would say, in 1967, "The Houston Ship Channel, in all frankness, is one of the worst polluted bodies of water in the nation. In fact, on almost any day this channel may be the most badly polluted body of water in the entire world." And in 1970, when a federal pollution panel inspected the ship channel, one member of the panel classed its waters as "too thick to drink and too thin to plow."

Jean Sulver saw all this long before. His *Ballades du Texas* (1937) includes a long poem titled "Le Chenal de Houston" in which he sees the ship channel again after apparently knowing it well as a boy or a young man. "Thank you, friend,/For taking me back there," he begins (translated from the French by André A. Crispin).

You say so, you are positive and doubt I wouldn't dare,
That this is the spot
We used to fish . . . ;
I believe you—because you told me—
But I cannot remember the bank so bare
These cropless fields
This naked lot;

The water seems deeper and the current swifter;
That noise, those thumps, these intermittent whistles
Are downright maddening . . . and it reeks of chlorine;

. . .

Jack, the fish are gone . . .
  One day the business bosses,
  Thin-lipped experts with horn-rimmed glasses,
  Came by these parts;

And talked and smoked,
And chewed and penciled,

And left again;

And then
Teams of khaki shirts
With teams of mules two by two
Poked in the mud,
Scratched all around,
Flattened the flowers,
Dug up the grass,
Mowed down the weeds

The mules ripped the fields with plows
Like those that paint the earth and bleed it;

And when everything was level and bland,
Cleansed and standardized,

They built, and built, and built,
And everything they bastardized.

Those horn-rimmed gents, horn-rimmed serpents
Rule the land

Nor is the ship channel alone, of course. The once lovely Clear Lake, near the Manned Spacecraft Center, was described in a Houston *Post* editorial in 1970, as "a pestilential, odiferous swamp, unfit for human use," as having "turned a slimy green from the sewage dumped into it," as "a prime example of how man, through carelessness, indifference and utter disregard for the welfare of his fellow mortals and of future generations, is destroying his environment." Call it another illustration of a grim but a needless paradox: the cost of success has been failure.

We have no style except what Nature has lent us. We put things cheek by jowl that no more belong together than catsup on caviar. Indeed, "It will all come out in the wash" would serve us faithfully, if not well, as a motto. And so it all does come out in the wash, as a rule leaving us crestfallen but still hopeful. Early in the century we asked A. C. Comey to propose a plan for our future. In 1913 we sent a man to Europe to study cities there and to report his *Findings and Recommendations for Houston's Guidance in Developing a Great Seaport City on the Gulf of Mexico.* Our population was less than a hundred thousand then; we could have made our future more habitable from that distance. We printed an interesting little book written by each man, Comey's in 1912 and Frank Putnam's in 1913. And that was that.

Then, in the 1920s (our population was 138,000 at the start of the decade, 292,000 at the end—still time) Will C. Hogg, one of our giants, spent part of his fortune to create the Forum of Civics, which tried to enrich our human environment. At the end of the period the Forum of Civics published an inspired but practical *Report of the City Planning Commission,* of which Hogg was the chairman. The report closed with this admonition from Hare & Hare, New York consultants: "It is the purpose of this plan to provide for the welfare, convenience and happiness of present and future citizens. In adopting the provisions of the plan, the people of Houston and their officials will have to decide whether they are building a great city or merely a great population." The report was published in 1929; Hogg died in 1930. And that was that.

Hogg was an extraordinary man. A son of the state's reform governor of the late nineteenth century, he was for many years the anonymous donor of thirty thousand dollars a year with which to buy crape myrtle plants for the city's parks and homes. Two tags went with each package of plants, one a pledge by the recipient to plant the shrubs on his grounds and the other giving explicit directions for planting and caring for the shrubs. When Hogg learned that Negroes were not getting the plants, he bought thousands more, which were given away only at Emancipation Park, then the Negroes' principal recreation center. Nearly everything Will Hogg did for the city was done anonymously, but only Sam Houston, who was Hogg's contradiction in nearly every way, looms larger in our past.

We will neither plan ahead nor even do much to contain the irritants of the present. More than most other big cities, perhaps more than any other, Houston suffers from a grave skin disease—billboards, signs, the bullying of freeway adscapes.

Houston lies behind the billboards. Call it sight pollution. To control or regulate this condition is unthinkable to us, though not for many other cities. Controls would inhibit our freedom— our freedom to sell advertising on billboards, our freedom to create ugliness, our freedom to make motoring more hazardous, our freedom to enlarge the vexations of urban life. We are vigilant to conserve our freedom; we are liberal in defining the word. Oddly enough, moreover, you can watch Houston with your ears, which is to say that our permissiveness about noise has made us tolerant of those gross and frightening noise makers, sirens and their more dreadful descendants. We like to call this cacophony the Houston serenade, but unlike our submission to billboards, this is an almost universal urban serenade. And therefore never phone to know for whom the siren cries; it cries for thee.

"What one misses most in Houston are old things," the Swiss journalist Paul Rothenhausler wrote in 1951. "After a few days [in Houston], one sings the praise of the past." It took a visitor to say it so well, and you wonder how many of us had ever missed old things. At the time he visited Houston, the city had preserved no structure from its past. Not until three years later, or nearly a century and a quarter after the city was begun, was a society formed to preserve the remaining architectural evidence of our past.

Houston is so new as a metropolis, and so eagerly continues to renew itself, the wonder is that *anything* old remains. Very little does. But, of course, though it is hard for us to see the past for the wonder and burdens and blunders of our present, not much ever existed that could now be old. Let us say that a structure built a century or more ago may fairly be called old. The subject is not Florence or London (Christopher Wren was born three centuries before the land for Houston was even surveyed) or Vienna but Houston, not even a century and a half old in 1970.

Our population was 2,396 in 1850, 4,845 in 1860, and 9,382 in 1870. What structures of consequence or likely to be preserved would be built in such a frontier town? Our population was 16,513 in 1880, and 27,557 in 1890, when Houston was

Manufacturing and heavy industry, part of the city's wealth, part of the city's pollution.

the fourth largest city in Texas after Dallas, San Antonio, and Galveston. Our population began really growing then, and the 1900 census put it at 44,648, making Houston the second largest city in the state. Not until the census of 1930 would Houston become the state's first city in population. Even when Houston was the capital of the Republic of Texas, from 1837 through 1839, nothing was built that would stand for long. The capitol itself, which would soon become a hotel, was not an edifice nor was it built of stone or planned by an architect. It was a hastily built frame structure, "painted peach blossom," Mary Austin Holley wrote at the time, one presumes with surprise.

Houston is not in the least a past-minded city. We have been late to preserve our past, as we have been late to plan for our future; we live in the present. What we do possess of our architectural past owes mainly to the Harris County Heritage Society, one of our most effective and worthy groups, and to a surprising and unexpected community effort to preserve some of the old buildings in what came to be called the Old Market Square area. Few houses or buildings are allowed to stand long enough to become old. When the lovely patina of age does get a chance to form, it is scrubbed away as though it soiled the city, or so it was deliberately removed in 1962 from the bronze of Sam Houston's equestrian statue in Hermann Park. We show little compassion for our city's past.

For one thing, our history does not call us back to the past as the histories of, say, Boston and Philadelphia and Athens do for their citizens. The Battle of San Jacinto, the decisive battle of the Texas Revolution, was fought four months before Houston was conceived and nine months before the village was in fact begun. The city never withstood or succumbed to an assault, and indeed no battle of any kind was ever fought in or for Houston. No Indian massacre ever occurred here. No plagues or fires or floods or hurricanes ever reduced the city.

Houston has been not so much a maker as a beneficiary of history, and disasters from which it has been mostly spared have served it well. Each of four wars, from the Battle of San Jacinto to World War II, and the great Galveston flood, in which six thousand perished, had important roles in the city's success. Yet the city does have a past of importance to complement a just-unwrapped appearance that seems free of any past more distant than the other day. Houston was the headquarters of the Confederate Trans-Mississippi Department, though one looks in vain for evidence of it. Before then, and more important, Houston was for a time the capital of the Reublic of Texas. But, like the capitol building mentioned earlier, the capital was built mainly of wood and canvas in a twinkling, designed not by architects but in haste by land speculators. And so no capital buildings of consequence ever existed to be preserved. With few exceptions—two, possibly three, houses and one small building—our past must be visually based in the last quarter of the nineteenth century.

The future? An unknown artist's conception, apparently painted in the 1930s, included giant downtown oil derricks in 1980. The other fantasy, "Houston 2000," was conceived for Foley's fiftieth anniversary in 1950.

The great fire of February 21, 1912, the most destructive in the city's history, swept through more than forty blocks of the old Fifth Ward, on the North Side.

■

A city creates its own myth, and each big city in a sense *is* a myth. Now a third dimension is forming slowly, like a graying, darkening sky, over reality and myth. The newer menace affects cities unequally, but Houston is among those most severely affected. The city, in which alone civilization was developed, came into existence more than five thousand years ago, or well before the dawn of history. The stunning changes then begun in human experience are called the Urban Revolution. Now, more than fifty centuries later, something else has occurred, as yet unnamed, to alter again man's condition of life.

The newer phenomenon may be seen most remarkably on the northeastern seaboard of the United States. But it can also be seen on the upper Gulf coast of Texas. This arc, reaching inland for up to a hundred miles, runs from Port Arthur on the east to Corpus Christi on the southwest, and its dimensions are expanding.

Forming within the arc is a city of cities, which is called a megalopolis. The word is nearly two thousand years old, for it was used in the first century A.D. by Philo Judaeus, the Alexandrian philosopher, "to describe the great city of ideas that predetermines and commands the material world in which we live." The quotation is from Jean Gottmann, the French geographer, who revived the concept in a book, *Megalopolis: The Urbanized Northeastern Seaboard of the United States.* The city of Houston is the capital of this smaller megalopolis, as New York is the capital of the larger one. And the Houston area has reacted to its new obligations much as the New York area has, proceeding culturally with indifference, even contempt, for the promised agonies of near and distant burdens.

Ibn Khaldun, an extraordinary man who happened also to be an Arab scholar, wrote *The Muqaddimah,* an introduction to history, in the fourteenth century. Among many values, *The Muqaddimah* remains, after six centuries, an inspired study of the culture of cities, notably as it reveals the nature of the everlasting dispute between rural and urban man. Ibn Khaldun saw cities as "centers of sedentary culture." The city, he said, is the only place where man can fulfill himself, which is a just evaluation unless you approve the iconoclastic wisdom of *Walden.* Only the city, Ibn Khaldun said, breeds arts and sciences and, indeed, all aspects of civilization.

"With language itself, [the city] remains man's greatest work of art," Lewis Mumford wrote in *The Culture of Cities,* where he quotes the judgment of Victor Branford and Patrick Geddes: "The central and significant fact about the city is that the city . . . functions as the specialized organ of social transmission. It accumulates and embodies the heritage of a region, and combines in some measure and kind with the cultural heritage of larger units, national, racial, religious, human. On one side is the individuality of the city—the sign manual of its regional life and record. On the other are the marks of the civilization, in which each particular city is a constituent element."

The city continues to be man's greatest communal enterprise, embodying the necessity of mass cooperation. On the other hand, of course, the city is to an even larger extent the executioner of individualism. The predominant aspect of urbanism is the necessity for group spirit; few urban men are islands. The city began a renewed surge in the tenth century, a burgeoning now intensified in megalopolitan growths in all sections of the industrialized world.

Mumford, the pre-eminent critic of urban society, is a New Yorker of exceptional gifts, few of them more considerable than his ability to write lucidly about the urban travail. "Ideally," he wrote in *The New Yorker* in 1956, "the unique task of the city is to bring together a multitude of economic and social activities within a limited area, for the enrichment of life by the continued interactions and transactions of varied groups of personalities."

An evaluation of a city's culture must say what is meant by culture, for it is a woolly, ambiguous word. The word is here taken to mean, perhaps in mild defiance of its etymology, the human environment. And by environment is meant a people's social, material, aesthetic, ethic, religious, and ritualistic experi-

Salvador Dali's surrealistic impression of Houston was a result of his visit to the city in 1952. The flaming giraffes, he said, symbolize oil derricks, at which a woman, her face covered with the camellias with which Houston is rich, looks with eager expectation. The port and the pioneers are shown in other symbols.

ence. A region's folk arts, its poetry, and the aspirations of its people are measures of its culture, but so too are its department stores, its hospitals, and athletics.

McCormick, in the pamphlet accompanying each of two British recordings of the Houston region's folk music, mentioned earlier, quotes Sam ("Lightnin'") Hopkins, a Houston Negro folk singer of large gifts and reputation. His statement would surprise, or even seem false, to the middle class that predominates in the region's population, men and women whose exposure to folk art has been limited to radio and television. That Houston lies on the edge of the blues country is obscured by our insularity, an insularity that is so peculiar in a port city and that tends to throw us a shade off center.

"The idea of it is that everybody 'round here plays music or makes songs or something," Hopkins said. "That's white peoples, colored peoples, that's them funny French-talking peoples, that's everybody, what I mean. They all of 'em got music." Hopkins saw a Houston unknown to many Houstonians, perhaps to the majority of Houstonians. Yet McCormick once told an acquaintance, "More Englishmen than Houstonians see Houston as a rich source of traditional lore, though otherwise the British think of Houston in cliches."

Who are these folk singers, these folk poets, some of whose work will live longer than the skyscrapers, most of whose work reflects something of the culture of the Houston megalopolis? Only Lightnin' Hopkins has overtaken fame.

Jimmy Womack, a handsome country boy who came to the city after being severely wounded in World War II, was a part-time television repairman here for years until he returned to Louisiana in 1961. A guitarist and singer, he is above all a composer of the traditional type of white-country ballads, as in "Atomic Energy":

Well, this modern world is quite the thing,
I'm sure you will agree,
Electric lights and gas and steam—
And atomic energy.

And several verses later:

I'm still looking for a town
Where I can find a face
Never heard of the atomic bomb
Nor belongs to the modern race.

Much of the region's past is deep-etched in song. One such, collected by the Lomaxes, was sung by Huddie ("Lead Belly") Ledbetter, a Negro convict and perhaps the most celebrated of colored folk singers. The song, titled "The Midnight Special," begins:

If you ever go to Houston,
You better walk right.
You better not stagger,
You better not fight.

Sheriff Binford will arrest you,
He will carry you down;
If the jury finds you guilty
You are Sugarland bound.

Some distant historian might conceivably piece together a history of the region from its folk music. Ed Badeaux, another collector of the Houston region's folk music, recorded "Wasn't It a Mighty Storm," a ballad of the 1915 hurricane, which begins:

In Galveston's a seawall
To keep the water down,
But the high tides from the ocean
Washed the water over the town.

By no means all Houston folk music is melancholy or bitter-sweet. Some is gay, some sassy. McCormick recalls a song sung by Blind Lemon Jefferson, an earlier Texas folk singer (one of his songs included the line "The blues came to Texas lopin' like a mule"), that begins:

I was born in Texas,
Schooled in Tennessee;
Ain't no woman
Can make a fatmouth out of me.

Something of the culture of the region is seen in the long sub-title of the McCormick albums: "A Panorama of the Traditions Found in Houston—the City and its Neighboring Bayous, Plains, Beaches, Prisons, Plantations, and Piney Woods." George Coleman, a stark, angular Negro of eccentric gifts, performs in both albums. Some future historian of the region would gain extra vision by reading the text of Coleman's "This Old World Is in a Terrible Condition." To hear him chant it, even on a phonograph record, is to be at length bewitched. Other performers include Paul Elliott, a Houston barber, a Bunyanesque storyteller whose subject is an alto saxophonist from, apparently, the fourth dimension, a man known as the Great White Bird; Linna Belle Hafti, a young grandmother who was married at the age of seventeen and soon thereafter, in 1936, moved to Houston; and John Lomax, Jr., a son of the nation's foremost collector of folk music.

6 • Houston, 1971.

7 • The Harris County Domed Stadium (the Astrodome).

Womack was born in Missouri, Coleman in a different world, Elliott in East Waco, Mrs. Hafti in Florida. One by one, some for weeks, some for good, they and others like them have cohered with Houston, making folk wisdom and experience indelible in song.

We like money, which affection we share with nearly everyone, but it is money that talks in our legends. Our folklore and our fairy tales are local Midas stories whose heroes made a fortune and held it. A man like Glenn H. McCarthy, who made one and lost it, whose rise to oil wealth and fall to the role of night club proprietor would elsewhere be held in memory as an object lesson in folly, merely disappears from our table of contents.

Facts—fewer millionaires live in all Texas than in Manhattan—fail to overcome a money myth. They say we altered the nursery rhyme to read "The butcher, the baker, the Cadillac maker." Lucius Beebe, to whom Cadillacs were Texas Volkswagens, wrote that a deceased Houstonian left forty-one Cadillacs, though in fact he left two. The Cadillac came to symbolize a life-style of opulence that was thought to typify Texas and especially Houston. A book was said to be titled *How to Live Like a Houstonian on $500 a Day*. The city appeared as the zenith, or perhaps the nadir, of the affluent society in fairy tales across the land, as though Houstonians were nearly all descended on the one side from Trimalchio and on the other from the Baron Munchausen. To give but one illustration, *The New Yorker* reported that "a particularly well-heeled Houston family [vacationing at a New Mexico fishing resort] assigned its uniformed maid the duty of catching every day's ration of fish."

The mythtakes bear long lives, yet the facts have been robust enough. One recalls the Houston woman who reported to police that her mink stole had been stolen—from her pickup truck. And the oilman who in 1946 sold part of his holdings for $54,000,000 and then gave each member of his family a million dollars in cash. And Roy M. Hofheinz, then the mayor of Houston, disclosing at a press conference in 1953 that he made his first million dollars by the time he was forty; though he was barely forty-one at the time, he was unable to say just when he had become a millionaire. "You just don't notice things like that," he said. And the rancher who gave his friends calendars showing twelve different color photographs of his young wife, one picture for each month of the year.

This presumed prevalence of plenty has attracted scoundrels, rogues, and cheats, some of them homemade, whose inventiveness often smacks of madness. Though our climate is mild indeed, many wealthy Houstonians once received a letter that should have been addressed to inhabitants of the arctic region. "I am taking bids," the writer said, "from several people on a mink bedspread. . . . The bidding will start at $10,000 if you desire the bedspread to be the only one in Texas, or at $25,000 if you desire the bedspread to be the only one in existence." A Tulsa man wrote to the Houston *Post* in 1965 to ask, "Is the heart of Houston big enough to stand another conterbution? If so send it to me. Do not worry about miss-appropriation. I want the money for my self." A city becomes known, even if briefly, as the Land of the Big Rich to its dismay.

A story, though far-fetched, reveals more about Houstonians' riches than all the facts. A Houston man, the story goes, was being questioned by a psychiatrist.

"What kind of car do you drive?"

"New Cadillac every year."

"Where do you live?"

"I live in a $150,000 house in Tanglewood."

"Where do you go on your vacations?"

"Spend a month or two a year traveling abroad."

"You seem to live a good life. What's your problem?"

"I make $150 a week."

One of the most revealing aspects of the Houstonian is that he is young. With a median age of 27.5 years (the figure is 35 for New York, 33 for Los Angeles, and 30 for Washington), our population is the youngest of America's big cities. But few who stand out have been or are young, and here I mean not alone those who stand out as heads of the symphony or the United Fund or the big corporations but as individuals. Nudists, vegetarians, and clairvoyants each have a club here, but I mean the kind of individualism that is a consequence of character and often of vigor and breadth of mind.

Perhaps it is our youth that causes us to move about within

the area so much more than seems sensible. And sometimes we take our houses with us. A European new to Houston marveled at the mobility of our houses. "If you see a house in Europe," he said, "even a small one, you know that it has stood exactly there throughout its life, whether it be twenty-five or two hundred and fifty years old. But almost any time I am out late at night in Houston, I find my car headed straight at a house in the middle of the street. Someone has decided to move it from the East Side to the Heights, or from one side of Main Street to the other." In fact, he was commenting on an old Texas custom.

The late Theodore Heyck's father was one of the early importers and shippers, whose headquarters were in Port Lavaca, where he built a mansion. When Galveston became the major Texas port, the senior Heyck transferred his operations. He had his home carefully razed and packaged and shipped, and rebuilt it in Galveston. But some time later the Heyck family had its first daughter. A gentleman of the old school, the father considered a seaport town entirely too rough a place to rear a young daughter and decided to move inland. Again he had the house torn down, shipped up river as far as possible, and then moved overland to Amarillo, deep in the Texas Panhandle. And there it stood as Amarillo's "old colonial mansion" until it burned in the 1930s.

Writing in 1377, Ibn Khaldun divided the world between rural nomads, the have-nots, and townsmen, the haves. The rural have-nots, he said, aspired to live in the towns, but the contented townsmen strove to exclude the unsophisticated rustics. In the long run, he said, the rustics succeeded in merging with the towns, doing so at first simply by capturing the towns and moving in. (The lesson that centers of sedentary culture are thus vulnerable still is worth remembering.) Even after six centuries have worked their changes, the dispute remains unchanged, though urban barriers have become so ineffectual as to be non-existent.

The swift development of the Houston megalopolis is a striking confirmation of the Arab's point. The megalopolitan growth became evident in the 1940s and, of course, still continues,

The most destructive modern storm affecting Houston was Hurricane Carla, which struck the Texas Gulf coast early in September 1961.

accelerated by the effects of the federal space laboratory. Some causes of the growth are diguised by the attractions of the region's lucky possession of a cornucopia, its abundant natural resources. For one thing, Texas offered immigrants of the mid-twentieth century the new chances and the new methods of the frontier. A frontier in spirit need not have the rusticity of a wild-west film; it can have skyscrapers and symphony orches-tras. "Houston is the kind of city men come to to get their best hold—a young man's town," the financier Robert C. Lanier said. (An educated man, and wealthy, he pronounced the word as it is customarily pronounced in this respect—"holt," not "hold.")

The population underwent a quick metamorphosis. Between 1940 and 1950 Texas changed from a rural to an urban state, a shift in character, attitudes, and aspirations that is far from completed. People moving into Texas moved into the cities, which was to be expected. But masses of people from the state's rural areas also moved to the cities, multiplying the cities' peril. As population swelled the cities, as the have-nots joined the haves, most of them to live in hope and die in despair, rural Texas was being drained, an exodus that continued through the 1960s. Between 1950 and 1960, the state's total population increased by 24 per cent. But the urban population increased by almost half while the rural population declined by a sixth. The ancient Arab was clairvoyant.

The exodus from rural areas is a national phenomenon with common causes, but in Texas, and notably in the Houston megalopolis, it was also impelled in other ways. The long drought ending in 1957 and the decline in cotton cultivation caused by the loss of foreign markets were large influences in forcing the state's farm tenants into the cities. Whatever the causes, the effects on the region's human environment of receiving such multitudes of rural immigrants are most obvious in the strengthening of the Calvinistic faiths and in the shock received by the educational system—the last most of all.

Texas was fancied to be filling with newcomers from the North after World War II, but it was no more than a fancy until the early 1960s. Texas has always been at least three-quarters full of Texans. Now, especially in the Houston megalopolis, the proportion of Texans is beginning to decrease. These immigrants are having a more subtle effect on the region's culture.

Who but a chauvinist would dare call Houston cosmopolitan? Yet the merging of so many diverse local and regional cultures, most of them coming to some extent from the traditions, customs, and ethics, and especially the ritualistic heritages, of Western Europe, direct the city away from its frontier character toward a larger share of life.

The majority of Texas Negroes live in the comparatively small area of the Houston megalopolis, and Houston itself has the state's largest concentration of Negroes. Nearly 400,000 Negroes live in the metropolitan area, or roughly one in five persons. In an article about Negro millionaires in Texas, *Ebony* magazine said, in 1952, "Houston is sometimes called the 'Bagdad of Negro America.'" And it is said also that Houston Negroes have a higher per capita wealth than the Negroes of any other American city. But such slogans and statistics give a false impression. Houston is no Elysian field for Negroes or, for that matter, for any ethnic group.

For Negroes, however, the Bagdad of Negro America has come far. Frederick Law Olmsted, one of the most important historical figures ever to make a critical appraisal of the area that was to become the Houston megalopolis, was in Houston in 1854. Writing of Houston in *The Cotton Kingdom*, an abridgement of his Southern trilogy of the 1850s, he said: "There is a prominent slave-mart in town, which holds a large lot of likely looking negroes, waiting purchasers. In the windows of shops, and on the doors and columns of the hotel, are many written advertisements, headed 'A likely negro girl for sale.' 'Two negroes for sale.' 'Twenty negro boys for sale,' etc."

The city is a conscious work of man; its destruction is often the unconscious work of man. As a man dies a little each day, so does a city. Anyone living in Houston during the decade following World War II experienced a metamorphosis from town to city that may never have been surpassed in speed and dimension except by Los Angeles. The spectacle, the excitement, were in the swift rise. It is an irony that such a rise contains the elements of a distant ruin that can be postponed, if not prevented, only by foresight.

"Most of our urban planning has failed," Lewis Mumford wrote in *The New Yorker*, "because it has been so limited and hasty that it merely stereotypes present disabilities instead of deleting them." Few cities seem to be able to adjust in any way except materially to the profound changes thrust upon man by the development of the megalopolis. No one has yet studied Houston as many of the nation's older cities have been studied. Houston is new, but it has never profited from its newness.

And so one returns to Olmsted for a glow—and for a warning. The quotation is from his book *A Journey through Texas*, and the point of it now lies in the last sentence:

"Since an English plough first broke the virgin sward of the sea-slope of Virginia, Saxons have not entered on so magnificent a domain [as Texas]. Many times, while making these notes, I have stopped to seek a superlative equal to some individual feature of the scenery . . . and one is more than ever wanting to apply to the country as a whole. . . . Texas . . . has an opulent future before her, that only wanton mismanagement can forfeit."

"*Urbes constituit aetas: hora dissolvit,*" Seneca wrote—"An age builds up cities: an hour destroys them."

"The fathers have eaten a sour grape, and the children's teeth are set on edge." So Jeremiah.

With so much against us, with so much to overcome because of our blunders and our prodigality, what is to commend us? If we return again, briefly, to the other side of that question, Henry James can start us toward an answer—toward the reasons many of us have affection for this city, reasons having little to do with O. W. Holmes's reminder that "The axis of the earth sticks out visibly through the centre of each and every town or city."

"Happiness," a matron wrote to the Houston *Post* in 1966, "is waking up in Houston on any normal hot and humid morning, and being told that night by your husband that he has been transferred back East." She enclosed with the unsigned letter a penny to "start a fund to help bring law enforcement, civilization, and culture" to Houston. The city could make many disparate replies to this angry woman. It could say that she was right, or it could say, "Nonsense!" The one reply would be as near the mark as the other, for a big city is, in fact, many cities. A white man who lives in the verdure of River Oaks is unlikely to be more than vaguely aware of the Houston known to a black man who lives in the foul and wretched Bottoms in the old Fifth Ward. A man who works in a plant on the Houston Ship Channel knows a quite different Houston from the one known to a clerk in Westbury Square, far to the northwest, or the Houston known to a man who ascends to work in a high-speed express elevator in a downtown skyscraper. Even the weather, if not the climate, may differ for each of the three.

Decades earlier Henry James said of another city: "It is difficult to speak adequately or justly of London. It is not a pleasant place; it is not agreeable, or cheerful, or easy, or exempt from reproach. It is only magnificent. You can draw up a tremendous list of reasons why it should be insupportable. The fogs, the smoke, the dirt, the darkness, the wet, the distances, the ugliness . . . You may call it dreary, heavy, stupid, dull, inhuman, vulgar at heart and tiresome in form." Even so, London was to him "on the whole the most possible form of life."

That is not to imply a comparison of Houston and London, but Houston too is big enough and troubled enough and more than sufficiently complicated to make it "difficult to speak adequately or justly" of the city. London grew gradually over the centuries, but Houston moved from wilderness to what may fairly be called bewilderness in a comparatively short time, thus adding pressures and tensions that could be managed more effectively by a city that grows little by little. A city endures such sudden growth to its additional peril.

Sight gives you your first impression. Houston meets the eye not only unaided by nature—by mountains or hills or any natural beauty except our wealth of trees—but to some extent disparaged by nature. "It is easy to explain why Houston lacks the exhilarating appeal to the eye of a San Francisco, a San Diego, or a Rio de Janeiro," W. D. Bedell has written. "It is flat. There is very little contrast for the eye to grab onto. The sun, especially in the summer, spews up from the trees to the east and sinks like a hot rock in the prairies to the west. There are only a few brief moments of long sun slants, of magically creeping shadows. Except in midtown there is little for the sun to hide behind, so all day, for endless hours, it seems to be directly overhead. The result is a sameness, in which height seems to be leveled out, and distance turns only into fuzziness."

On the other hand, and what usually strikes the newcomer if few Houstonians, the city is so clean, and not alone from its newness. Indeed, a building remains clean and new-looking long after it is built. The ten-story City Hall, completed in 1940, and the nineteen-story Mellie Esperson Building, completed in 1941, both are faced with white stone. Three decades later both were still white. Our streets are clean; our downtown sidewalks are hosed at night. An Ohio native who lived here for many years at last returned to Ohio for a visit. He took his teen-age son, who was born in Houston, to show the boy for the first time what the father had for so long praised. The boy was shocked and dismayed by the grubbiness of his father's native industrial city; the father saw Houston for the first time.

The Mad Driver—once part of the entrance to the garage of the Petroleum Building, and more and more a faithful symbol.

And the city conveys both a sense of energy and of excitement, as though a long and jubilant festival was to start in just a few days. Perhaps you can see that last more clearly from a distance—from Paraguay, say. "Houston, Houston, Houston, Houston, Houston! That's all I hear." So spoke, but in Spanish, a Paraguayan in a family tape recording sent to his granddaughter, who was attending a Houston high school as an exchange student. No doubt he meant the moon, the heart, and the domed stadium. Only the first of those disparate ventures is likely to be more than a temporary phenomenon, but each was surely a part of the Paraguayan's news.

You return again and again to what may be the main source of our burdens to see what must be achieved to overcome those things that more and more cause the urban mind and spirit to flag, but that the people are helpless to oppose as individuals. So swift, so dramatic, has been the rise of Houston since the Second World War that the city's newer dimensions are rarely comprehended. The Houston metropolitan area is considerably larger than the state of Rhode Island. And the same area is larger in population than each of fifteen states. Indeed, the four states of Vermont, Delaware, Wyoming, and Nevada have a combined population smaller than that of Houston—but they are represented by eight United States senators. Roughly the size of Warsaw, Stockholm, Singapore, Naples, Bucharest, Brussels, or Munich, Houston had to adjust to—to make do for—such a population in a hurry rather than little by little.

The leader who would seriously propose the creation of a Houston Depopulation Commission would be thought a madman, so perhaps we need a center for urban idealism, and the energy and inspiration to give effect to that idealism. And the phrase urban idealism must be taken as a way to make the city more comfortable, more peaceful for humans, a city in which the shocks and the stridence and the absurdities of urban life are somehow reduced.

■

Nearly two million of us live in the Houston metropolitan area, swiftly civilizing our rural landscape. This refuge for woolgathering has not yet perished, but ex-rural marks the spot.

Main Street, looking north from Congress, probably in 1882, when two blocks of the street were paved for the first time—unsuccessfully, it would develop—with limestone blocks laid on gravel. The piles of what seem to be rubble apparently are the paving blocks.

Since then more than a quarter of the city's surface has been paved—too successfully, it has developed—with concrete freeways, expressways, cloverleaf puzzles, roads, and streets, and with concrete and asphalt plains, niching hosts for automobiles at rest. The American General Building, masking its pave in the rear, is in the foreground.

The Century of the Common City. From this, at left above, the fresh air of lower Main Street, c. 1870 . . .

To this, at left below, the beginning of fouled air on lower Main, c. 1921 . . .

To this, above, the smog of 1970.

And we have our bibles—one for God . . .

and one for mammon.

Sunday afternoon in 1900 (Sam Houston Park), above.

Sunday afternoon in 1970 (the Astrodome), at right.

A few of us live like this, in River Oaks.

And like this, in the Memorial area.

Many more of us live like this.

And like this.

But most of us live like this.

In 1870 we lived in these houses (probably Texas Avenue at
Austin Street).

In 1970 we lived in these houses.

And some of us lived in houses like this one, the home of
Mr. and Mrs. André A. Crispin.

We have parks (a fountain in the
northwestern corner of Hermann
Park), at left, and parks
(a Negro playground), below.

The nineteenth-century Gothic architecture of the St. John Evangelical Lutheran Church (1890), below, and the Greek revival style of the Nichols-Rice-Cherry House (c. 1850), at right, stand in eloquent contrast before the high-rise masses of the middle twentieth century. The church and the house are among several structures removed to the Sam Houston Historical Park to form a museum of Houston's past. This is the work of the Harris County Heritage Society; indisputably, the most effective organization of its kind in the city's history.

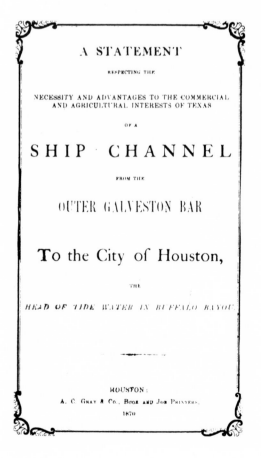

The Port of Houston, c. 1859, above. At left is the cover of an 1870 pamphlet, the second to be published with the hope of bringing the sea fifty miles inland to Houston.

At right, the port in 1970.

The port, as painted by Richard Stout in 1965.
—From the collection of Mr. and Mrs. Meredith Long

Connecting the port with the Gulf of Mexico is the Houston Ship Channel, the city's access to the world.

Nothing had so large an effect on the city's character as the presence of the Manned Spacecraft Center of the National Aeronautics and Space Administration. The center gave us a bond with the old ports of western Europe that played leading roles in the great exploration voyages of two, three, and four centuries before. The center informed the city with two excitements, one the race for the moon and beyond, the other intellectual. Technical direction of America's space effort comes from Houston.

The lunar module, above, rests on the center's simulated moonscape. Astronaut equipment is being tested at right above, and what may be called a space junkyard—obsolete spacecraft— appears at right below.

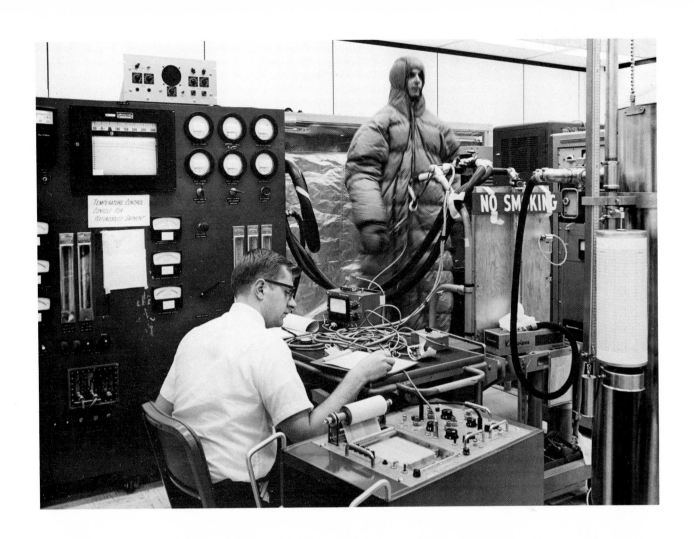

The Manned Spacecraft Center's public exhibits, above, attracted crowds long before a moon rock was displayed. Next to the center is the Lunar Science Institute, sponsored by a consortium of forty-eight universities, which was dedicated in 1970. The institute is housed in the old J. M. West mansion, on whose grounds are the gazebos at left. The main hall of the institute, a center for space research, is at right.

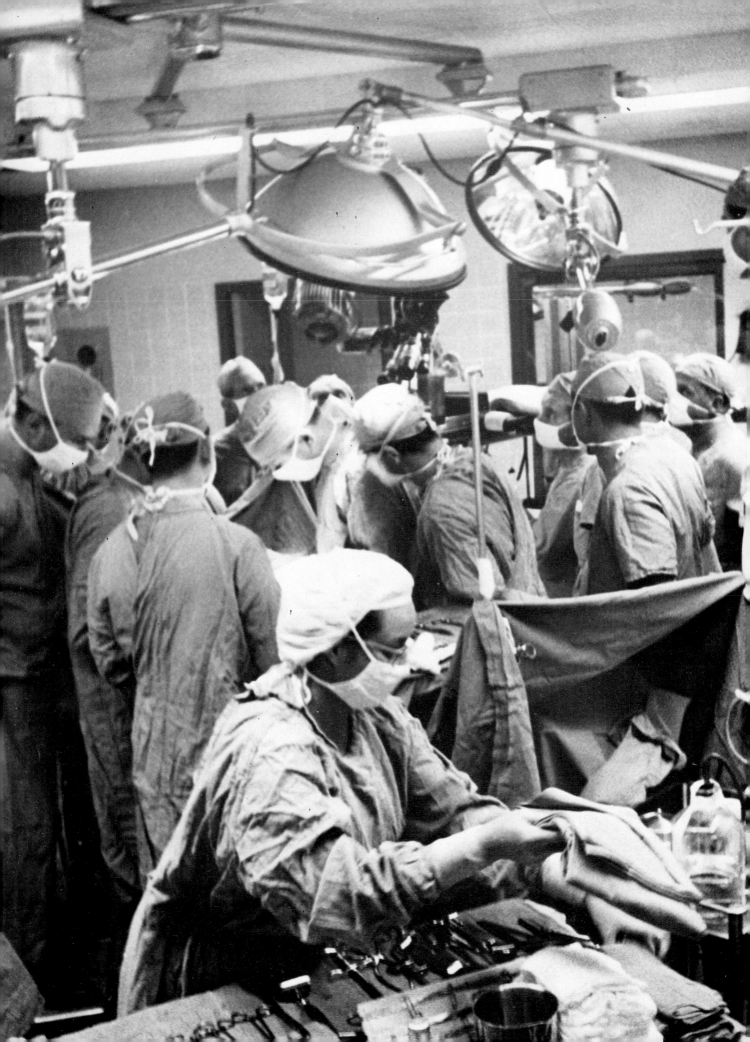

One of the superlatives of Houston life is the Texas Medical Center, where more human heart transplants have been made than in any other city in the world. Its patients come from all the earth to have arteries patched with Dacron, to have artificial valves implanted in hearts, even to receive new hearts. And not alone the heartsick, though the marvels worked first by Dr. Michael E. DeBakey and then by DeBakey and Dr. Denton A. Cooley put the Texas Medical Center into the world's focus. On the left, Dr. Cooley is shown during a heart-transplant operation. Dr. DeBakey is shown above. Below, Dr. Cooley plays the bass fiddle in the Heartbeats, a dance orchestra composed of doctors.

The sixty-one members of the Houston Automobile Club owned two-thirds of the eighty horseless carriages here in 1906, which is believed to be the date of the photograph shown above. By 1970, right, Houston had unfortunately become the leading car-use city in the United States. Baltimore and Houston were almost exactly the same size in 1962, when Houston had 64 per cent *more* automobiles than Baltimore.

Our first traffic signals appeared in 1921—police-
operated stop-and-go signals at eleven downtown
intersections, as at Main and Franklin, above. Half
a century later it was done as you see on the right.

And for petrochemicals . . .

And for our port . . .

And for our livestock, but especially cattle. The scene of the cattle auction above is Gus S. Wortham's Bar 9 Ranch . . .

And for cotton, which we do grow, even in Harris County, but which has been more important to us as something we move—even much earlier than the scene in the yards at the Southern Pacific's Grand Central Depot, below, in 1894 . . .

And especially for rice. Irrigation has made Harris County a rice producer of importance, and more than a quarter of the nation's rice is grown within a hundred-mile radius of Houston.

We make candles, notably at the Faroy plant, above. In 1950, when Preston Frazier and Addison McElroy started Faroy, they made fewer than a thousand candles in McElroy's garage. In 1969, by then filling a large and handsome plant, Faroy made 5,791,262 candles, among other things, which were sold throughout the world.

And we make chemicals. The combination of our ship channel, immense natural resources, and the fact that the product of one chemical plant is often the raw material of another created on the banks of the ship channel one of the world's greatest concentrations of petrochemical industries.

This is the oil business.

And so is this, above—the office of K. S. "Bud" Adams, Jr.,
who also owns Houston's professional football team, the Oilers.

And for commerce common to all cities, which is to say for
four things, construction . . .

And garage sales . . .

And art galleries (the DuBose Gallery) . . .

And manufacturing (members of the board of directors of
the Sinclair-Koppers Chemical Co. tour the concern's Houston
plant).

First we wanted immigrants to hurry. Read the lure on this broadside, c. 1876: "Over 30,000,000 ACRES OF LANDS . . . Over 200,000 Settlers in Texas Last Year!!"

A century later we wanted everyone to take it easy.

Texas Land EXCURSION!

Take a trip with us to where happy farmers are picking strawberries every day, while we fellows are suffering 20 below zero

March 5th, 1907.

From Minneapolis, Minn., Our tickets permit stop over any, where both ways and side trips in Texas, to any point for half fare for round trip . . . . **To Houston Texas.**

At Houston we will show you beautiful prairie lands, fanned continually by soft Gulf breezes, at **$16.00** to **$25.00** per acre, on easy terms.

This section of Texas has abundant rainfall, healthy climate, good soil, pure water, and on account of its nearness to the sea, it has both warm winters and cool summers.

These lands grow **$60.00** worth of Rice per acre; **75** bushels of oats per acre; **50** bushels Corn per acre; **$200.00** to **$400.00** worth of berries and vegetables per acre; **$400.00** of figs per acre, all other crops in proportion and can grow something every month in the year; oranges and lemons grown here successfully too. These lands lay as fine as Central Illinois, covered with prairie grass, 2 feet high, fine oak timbers along the banks of all streams.

Thousands are going to **TEXAS** **Land Values advancing by Leaps and Bounds.**

Go now, do not delay, **$27.50** for round trip. Send us the money for ticket today. If you can't go, money will be refunded.

Large Tracts For Syndicates,
Small Tracts For Settlers.

Don't waste time writing for maps and price lists, just get ready for... **March 5th**

⌀ GET READY! ⌀

Should you be unable to come to Minneapolis, or wish to go direct to Houston, then buy home-seekers ticket to Houston and call for CHAS. O. ELWOOD, or, A. C. SWANSON, at Rice Hotel, Houston, or, at room 402, Mason Bldg., Houston. Always notify Minneapolis Office, when you start.

Take Notice! Remember Texas is a thousand miles across, in almost any direction and consequently room for all kinds of climates and soils. Snow sometimes is falling at some place in Texas, on the same day we are picking strawberries in Houston. So don't be deceived, go direct to HOUSTON, in the GULF COAST COUNTRY.

ELWOOD LAND CO.
718 Guaranty Loan Bldg.,
MINNEAPOLIS, ⌀ **MINNESOTA.**

We were zealous in seeking immigrants a century ago; even half a century ago. Read the bait on a poster advertising a Minneapolis-to-Houston land excursion of 1907: "Take a trip with us to where happy farmers are picking strawberries every day, while we fellows are suffering 20 below zero." Later we would need a depopulation commission.

But the immigrants came—by the hundreds, then by the thousands, at last by tens of thousands. And many have formed their own communities within the city, as have the Chinese, who have their own Baptist church.

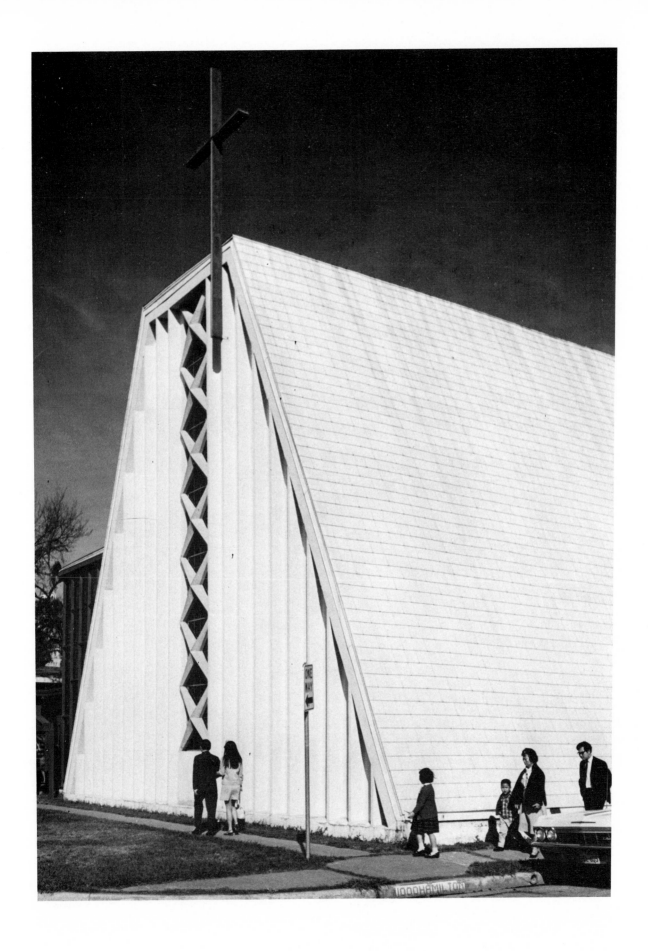

We have around 1400
churches, including the First
Presbyterian . . .

And the First Pagan.

"The more things change, the more they are the same." A cemetery for humans, at right and above, and the Houston Pet Cemetery, at left.

The City Hall at left (behind it are the Sam Houston
Coliseum and the Music Hall) . . .

And part of City Hall's domain.

Much more than architectural style had changed in the theater by the time the world-famous Alley Theater moved to its new structure, above, in 1968.

What a pity that most of our too few parks are in the more fashionable southern and western sections of the city, where they are needed the least! Our largest park, the 1466-acre Memorial, lies between River Oaks and Tanglewood and the huge Memorial area; residential areas that are themselves parks. Hermann Park, above (in a rare dressing of snow and ice), lies to the west, but too many of its 410 acres have been parceled out to worthy projects that might have been put elsewhere, notably a planetarium and natural science museum and the pavement for their parking areas.

Miller Memorial Theater, Hermann Park

The Rice Hotel opened in 1913. This has been the site of a hotel since 1840, and until then the site of the capitol of the Republic of Texas.

The Warwick Hotel (the glass elevator ascending on the right) opened in 1926, reopened in 1964 after being purchased, elaborately remodeled, and enlarged by John Mecom.

We eat at hundreds of restaurants and cafés, a few of them distinguished. Brennan's, for one, at left (the patio), our most beautiful restaurant; or Maxim's, above (the wine room); or, for different reasons, Antone's, below, as celebrated for its Po' Boy sandwiches as Maxim's is for its Red Snapper Excelsior or rack of lamb or a whole poached sea trout . . .

Or at our most distinguished steak house, Brenner's, at left (looking out on the garden-village entirely built by Herman Brenner over many years); or soul food, below; or even in tree houses, below left, at the undeniably unique Los Troncos Restaurant.

In Old Market Square, a restored section of the older part of the central city: The Buffalo Bayou Flea Mart, above, is a maze of shops beneath the old Magnolia Brewery Building (c. 1893). The main dining room, right, and the handsome and authentic split-stairway entrance of the Bismarck Restaurant confirm the original architectural style of the Magnolia Brewery.

A century of Houston architecture: The detail of the Morris Building, below (c. 1869), shows what may have been the first iron-front building in Houston. The building was on the east side of Main between Congress and Preston.

The Houston Post Building, at right, opened in 1970.

This, the Houston Academy, c. 1869, was the whole school system when it was opened in 1859.

This, opened in 1969, is the central administration building of the Houston Independent School District.

Rice University (the Quad).

The University of Houston.

The great hall of the Museum of Natural Science.

The children's zoo, part of the Hermann Park Zoo.

Louis Paulham, a barnstorming French aviator, brought the spectacle of manned flight to Houston in February 1910, top. A year later Houston held its first aviation meet, above and below.

Any of these airships could fly inside the Houston Intercontinental Airport buildings, opened in 1969, right.

160

Our taste in sculpture would seem to have changed indeed. The Brownie, as the drinking fountain above was known when it was put in Sam Houston Park in 1907, now stars in the children's zoo. The fifty-ton *Abesti Gogora V,* right, by Eduardo Chillida, was brought to the south lawn of the Museum of Fine Arts in 1966.

An unfinished sketch (1966), left, by John Biggers; the Humble Building is in the background.

Biggers, a man of large gifts, once noted "the elegance of the great storage bins," above, which stand near Buffalo Bayou near the city's core. "The simplicity of the architecture," he said. "Those great bowls standing there loaded with food. Thomas Mann wrote about the great storehouses in Egypt preparing for seven years of famine. When I see them, that's what I think of. They always keep them pure white. The real meaning of grandeur. I just hope that these things don't get cluttered up. They humanize the environment."

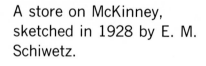

A store on McKinney, sketched in 1928 by E. M. Schiwetz.

At Lynchburg Ferry on the Houston Ship Channel, sketched in 1929 by E. M. Schiwetz.

Main at Congress in the
early 1930s, sketched by
E. M. Schiwetz.

Main at Prairie in the
early 1930s, sketched by
E. M. Schiwetz.

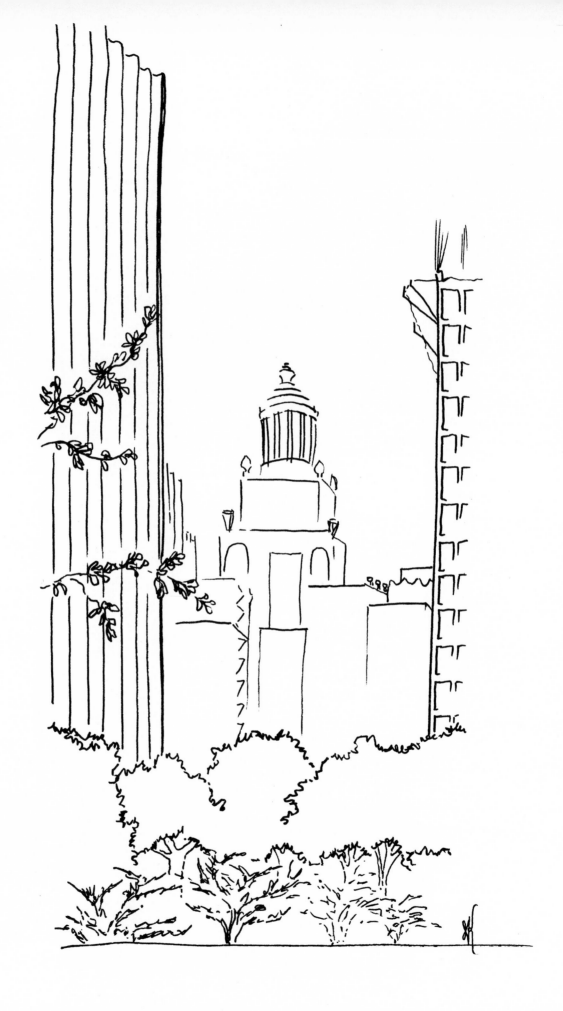

168

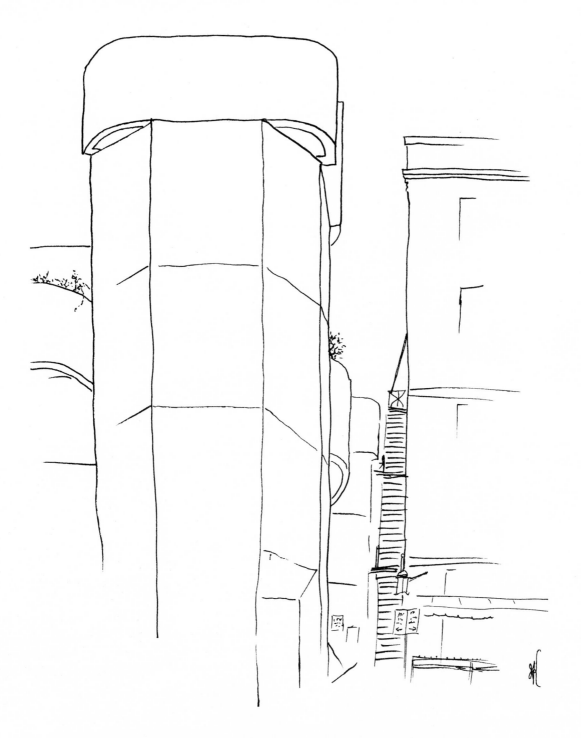

If the skyline had an architectural symbol from 1927 into the
1960s, and perhaps afterward, it would have been the tower
of the forty-foot Corinthian columns atop the thirty-two-story
Niels Esperson Building, shown at left flanked by the Houston
Lighting and Power Company Building and One Shell Plaza.
Sketched by Jeannette Klemola.
Above, a corner of the Alley Theater.
Sketched by Jeannette Klemola.

Post Oak Galleria, a shopping center whose lower level is an ice-skating rink.

At right, "The Broken Obelisk," a three-ton steel sculpture, twenty-six feet high, by Barnett Newman, dedicated to Martin Luther King. The sculpture stands at the Rothko Chapel, opened in 1971, a separate part of the Institute of Religion. The ecumenical chapel was built to house the last great works of Mark Rothko: three vast triptyches and five panels with a mystic or religious theme. The sculpture, the chapel, and the paintings, together one of the city's glories, were given to Houston by Mr. and Mrs. John de Menil.

Hippies in Hermann Park,
above left, and the
continuing line-up at
James Coney Island,
below left.

A ball in Cullinan Hall, the
Museum of Fine Arts.

Water: Part of the Mecom Fountain, above; a fountain in Westbury Square, below, a singular shopping center with a peculiar and arresting kind of magic at night. The waterfall in the bird house at the zoo, right.

is this—a labyrinth of underground pedestrian tunnels flanked by shops, snack bars, and businesses. Is it raining downtown? Then you can, if you know your way, go for blocks without coming up for a shower.

Two sculptures, one of them innocent. *Hercules Upholding the Heavens* above, is at the Museum of Fine Arts. The water tower, left, is at the Manned Spacecraft Center.

Our rain season may run from January to December, but normal
rainfall is around forty-five or forty-six inches a year.

And sometimes it snows in Houston—every ten years, a legend says.
Once, in 1859, we even had a white Christmas.

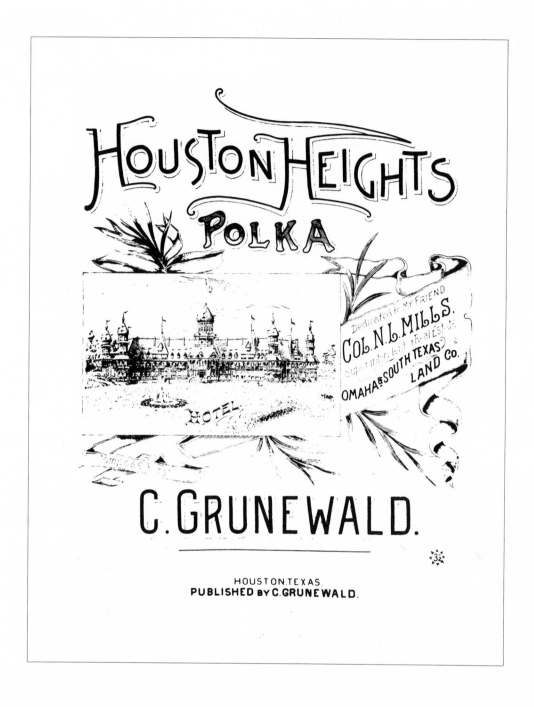

Time *is* visible. The cover of the sheet music for an 1893 polka marked the city's pace then, as did the ad, at right, for the city's most celebrated barber shop, Norris of Houston, three-quarters of a century later. (Norris Womack, the owner, is at the top of the pile of barbers.)

INDEX

Page numbers shown in **bold face** indicate illustrations.

COLOR ILLUSTRATIONS
(following page 48)

1. Texas Avenue at Crawford, looking west. By Bill Condon.
2. West Dallas Avenue, a Negro tenement area near the city's core. By John Biggers.
3. Old Market Square, Travis Street. By Herbert Mears.
4. The skyline from Capitol Avenue Bridge, painted in 1948 by E. M. Schiwetz.
5. The Jesse H. Jones Hall for the Performing Arts.
6. Houston skyline, 1971.
7. The Harris County Domed Stadium (the Astrodome).